Excel

Basic Skills

Basic Reading Skills

Years 1–2

Ages 6–8

Get the Results You Want!

Peter Howard

PASCAL PRESS

Reprinted 2006, 2007, 2008 (twice), 2009, 2010, 2011, 2013, 2014, 2015, 2016, 2018, 2020, 2022, 2024, 2026

ISBN 978 1 74125 165 4

Pascal Press
PO Box 250
Glebe NSW 2037
www.pascalpress.com.au

Publisher: Vivienne Joannou
Edited by Christine Eslick
Page layout and typesetting by Typecellars Pty Ltd
Cover by DiZign Pty Ltd
Printed by Vivar Printing/Green Giant Press

Contents

Introduction

In today's world, most children probably read less than their parents or grandparents did at the same age. Distractions such as television and video games take up many hours that could be spent reading. To excel in reading requires plenty of practice.

The ***Excel*** Basic Skills Basic Reading Skills series is a three-book set of workbooks for Years 1–2, 3–4 and 5–6 which aims to give primary school children this important practice in reading and understanding using a variety of accessible texts. Each varied one-page exercise should not take more than about **15 minutes**. Most pages have questions that require one-word answers. These words are found in the text or on the page. This ensures that a child must concentrate hard and read every word.

In this first book in the series, *Basic Reading Skills Years 1–2*, the activities cover a wide range of reading skills such as:

- basic comprehension of a text
- predicting words in a story
- recognising different 'voices' in a text
- finding words that are wrong
- sorting different kinds of words.

Fun activities, such as anagram puzzles and simple crosswords, are also included.

Parents and teachers are advised to remove the answers from the centre of the book. When correcting a child's work, it is important to explain any errors that have been made.

Which cat has no tail?

The only cat that has no tail at all is the Manx cat. It gets its name from where it was first bred. This was an island in the Irish Sea—The Isle of Man.

One kind of Manx cat, the 'stumpy', has a very short tail. The 'rumpy' is the one without any tail.

The rumpy's body is small and it has a round head. Its back legs are longer than the front ones. When the rumpy Manx cat runs, it looks like a rabbit on the move.

Use a word from the story to fill each space.

1 A stumpy Manx cat has a ____________ tail.

2 A ________________ Manx cat has no tail at all.

3 The heads of Manx cats are ____________________.

4 A rumpy looks like a ___________________ when running.

5 Which word means the same as **sort**? ________________

Which is the slowest animal?

The slowest animal in the world is the sloth. It lives in the South American jungle. Most of the time it hangs upside down from the branch of a tree. When it moves, it will slowly pull itself along the branch, to look for leaves to eat.

To find another tree, the sloth slowly climbs down. It drags itself even more slowly along the ground. It might take ten minutes to travel twenty metres. It gradually climbs up the new tree. It rests for a long time before it begins eating again.

Use a word from the story to fill each space.

1 A sloth is the ______________ animal.

2 It usually hangs upside ____________________.

3 It eats ________________________.

4 Trees that sloths climb are in the ______________________.

5 Which word means the same as **relaxes**?

____

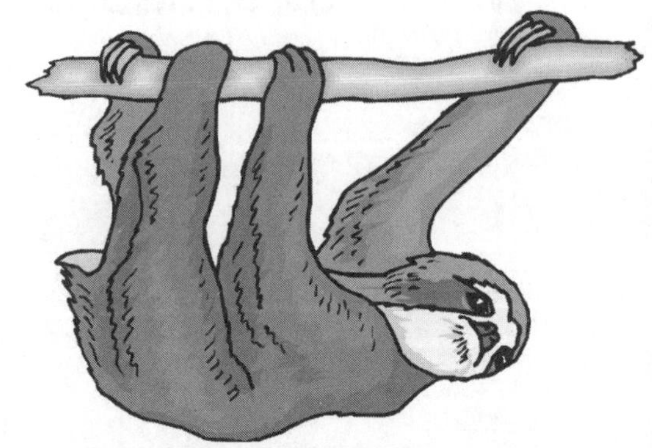

Missing words 1

One word is missing in each line where there are four dots. Write the word that you think should be there.

Long ago the world was f.... of animals. 1 ______________

They l.... on plains and in forests. Today 2 ______________

many animals have less and l.... space 3 ______________

to live in. People have m.... new villages. 4 ______________

T.... and cities have grown larger. 5 ______________

Trees in the jungle have been c.... down. 6 ______________

Wood is needed to m.... paper or build 7 ______________

houses for all of u.... . 8 ______________

Now there are n.... many wild tigers, 9 ______________

pandas, gorillas a.... other apes left. 10 ______________

Besides having nowhere t.... live, these 11 ______________

animals are hunted by m.... who sell 12 ______________

their skins.

How many eyes has a fly?

A fly has only two eyes but each eye has hundreds of tiny lenses. This means that a fly can see all around a room at the same time.

It is hard to creep up on a fly and try to swat it. The fly can see your hand even if you come from above or behind.

Flies are useful. They get rid of all kinds of dead animals. They lay eggs that hatch into maggots. Maggots eat up dead bodies.

In a house or home they have bad habits. They dribble on food lying about. Make sure that all food is covered and flyscreens on doors and windows are in place.

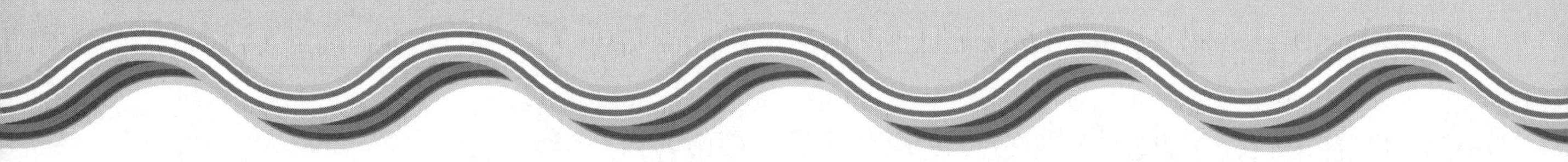

Use a word from the story to fill each space.

1 A fly's eye has many ______________.

2 Flies can ____________________ all around the room.

3 ________________________ eat dead things.

4 Flyscreens are used on windows and ________________________.

5 Which word means the same as **small**?

____

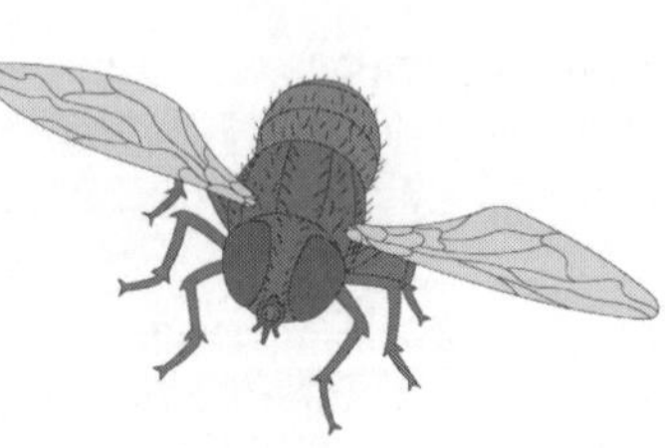

Do animals talk?

Animals can talk to each other using simple sounds. Monkeys make the most sounds with different meanings. Monkeys also make lots of different faces to show how they feel.

We think that insects can talk in their own way. Bees live happily together in a hive. There is much work to be done. Honey is made. Babies have to be fed. How would they do all this without some way of talking?

When one ant finds food, in no time many others arrive. How was the ant able to tell others about his find?

Use a word from the story to fill each space.

1 The most sounds are made by ________________.

2 We think bees must do some ________________.

3 What is a bee's home called? ________________

4 What insect might tell others about food?

____

Who is speaking? 1

Read each sentence. Write who is speaking in the space. Choose answers from the box.

chef	**nurse**	**driver**	**teacher**
clown	**mother**	**beggar**	**farmer**

1 Can you spare some money? ____________________

2 I like the feel of this car. ____________________

3 Don't forget to clean your teeth. ____________________

4 I shall cook a lovely dinner. ____________________

5 How do you like my big red nose? ____________________

6 My wheat crop needs some rain. ____________________

7 Now you must all look at the board. ____________________

8 The doctor will see you soon. ____________________

Which animal is the river horse?

The river horse is the hippopotamus. When it is swimming in a lake or river, it shuts its nose and ears and sinks down to the bottom. It then finds it easy to walk along like a giant horse. Besides being a kind of river horse, it is almost like a submarine.

This animal has the largest mouth of any animal except the whale. When the mouth is open, it looks like a red cave. The hippo must leave the water to eat. At night it finds green crops growing nearby. Its stomach is not filled until it has swallowed at least 150 kilograms of food.

Use a word from the story to fill each space.

1 The hippo walks like a giant ____________________.

2 Only the ____________________ has a larger mouth.

3 What colour is the inside of its mouth? ____________________

4 What colour is the food it eats? ____________________

5 Which word means the same as **closes**?

____

Cruel games hurt others

Some boys were playing in a field near a pond. When they were tired of running about, they picked up stones. They began throwing them at frogs in the pond.

At last an old frog put its head out and said: 'Boys, do you know what you are doing? This may seem fun to you, but a stone can easily kill us. We don't think it is much fun. How would you like it if that horse over there came and decided to kick you for fun?'

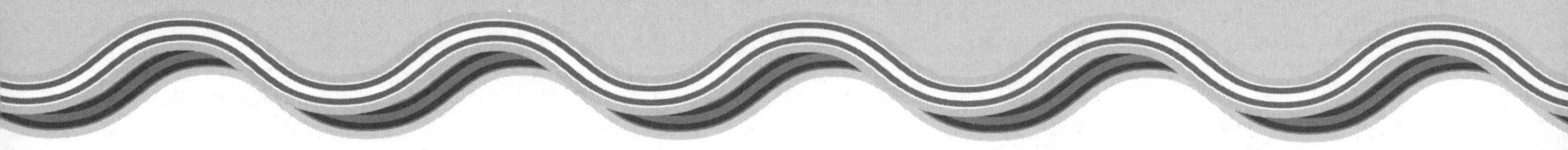

Tick the box against each sentence that is true.

1 A group of boys and girls were playing. ☐

2 The boys threw stones at a horse. ☐

3 The boys aimed at frogs in the pond. ☐

4 One frog thought it was a big joke. ☐

5 The old frog was upset. ☐

Crossword puzzle 1

Write the answers in the puzzle using the clues below. Each word has the 'a' sound like in 'cat'. Write the answers again below next to the clues.

Across

2 I hold things with my ____________________.

4 Soot is always ____________________.

6 A king is a ____________________.

7 A flag will ____________________ in the wind.

8 I have a ____________________ between each tooth.

Down

1 I put on a ____________________ when I am out in the sun.

3 A cloth that is a bit wet is ____________________.

4 A gun goes off with a ____________________.

5 We can have a ____________________ as a pet.

What is a trap-door spider?

The trap-door is a spider that makes a kind of tunnel into the ground. It covers the entrance with a lid or trap-door. This lid is made of a mixture of mud and the silk that the spider spins. The door is fixed to the tunnel by silk hinges.

People think that the trap-door is as dangerous as the funnel-web spider. Trap-door spiders do not harm us. They eat insects that attack plants and flowers. The clever trap-door spider waits near the door. When an insect passes by, it opens the door. It quickly snatches the insect and then with one bite it injects a poison. Now it can enjoy a meal.

Use a word from the story to fill each space.

1 A trap-door spider digs a ______________.

2 It makes a ____________________ of mud and silk.

3 Trap-door spiders do not ________________________ us.

4 They make a meal of an ________________________.

5 Which word means the same as **grabs**?

____

Change the first letter 1

The first letter of a word in each sentence is wrong. Write the word correctly in the space.

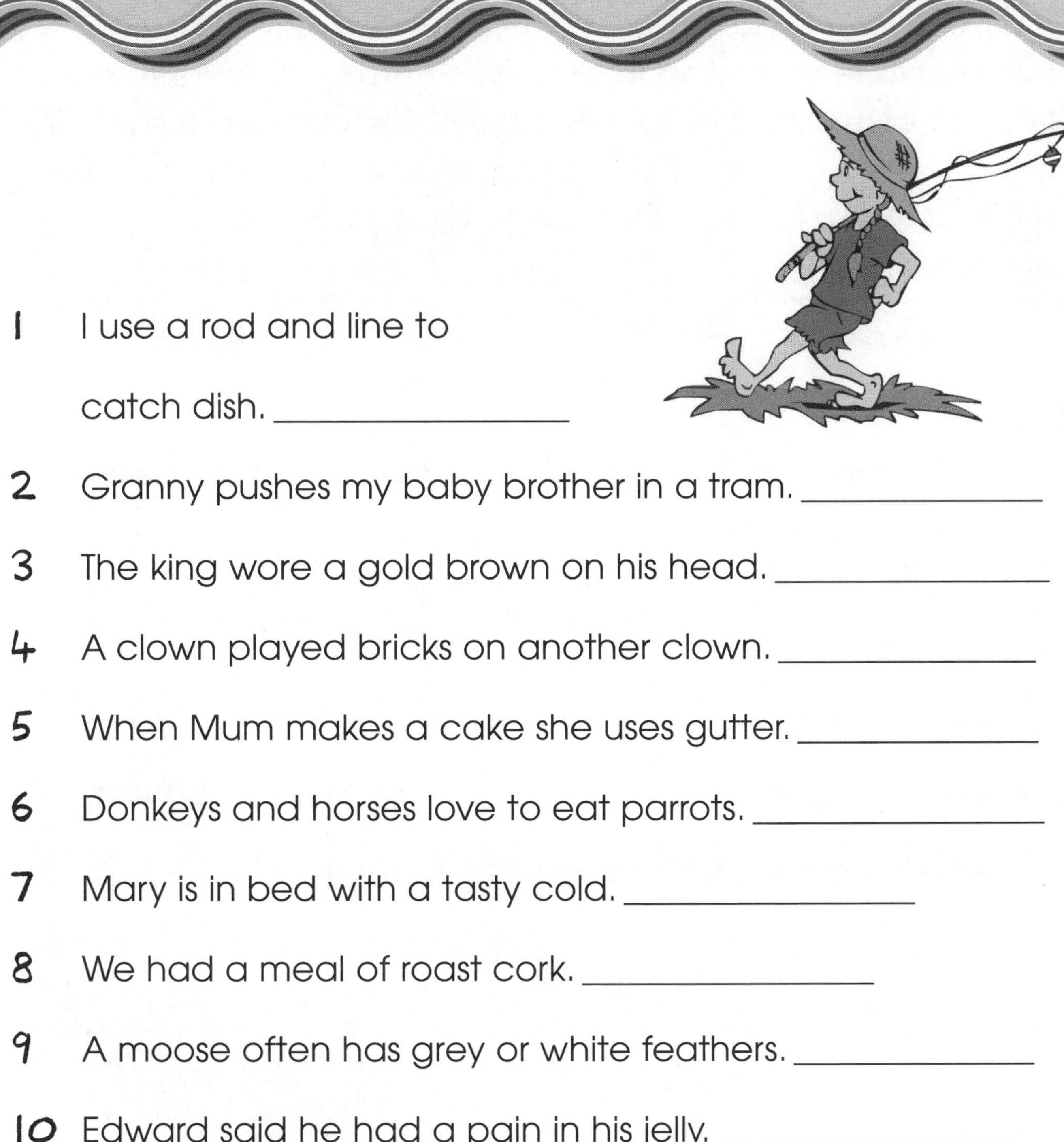

1 I use a rod and line to catch dish. ________________

2 Granny pushes my baby brother in a tram. ____________

3 The king wore a gold brown on his head. ____________

4 A clown played bricks on another clown. ____________

5 When Mum makes a cake she uses gutter. ____________

6 Donkeys and horses love to eat parrots. ____________

7 Mary is in bed with a tasty cold. ________________

8 We had a meal of roast cork. ________________

9 A moose often has grey or white feathers. ____________

10 Edward said he had a pain in his jelly. ________________

Which was the largest dinosaur?

The largest dinosaur was *Brachiosaurus.* It was as high as the roof of a small house. It was as long as four taxi cabs end to end. It was as heavy as seven fully grown elephants.

Brachiosaurus lived about 150 million years ago. It spent much of its time wading in swamps. There it could keep away from other fierce dinosaurs that did not know how to swim. If it did come to a fight, *Brachiosaurus* could bite with its large teeth and use its huge long tail to knock down other dinosaurs.

Use a word from the story to fill each space.

1 *Brachiosaurus* was a large ______________________.

2 It lived 150 ________________ years ago.

3 *Brachiosaurus* liked to wade in ________________.

4 It had a huge long ____________________.

5 Which word means the same as **home**?

____

How many humps has a camel?

A camel from Arabia has one hump. It is called a dromedary. A camel from Asia has two humps. This camel is a Bactrian. These two kinds of camel mate and have babies. When the babies grow up they are called crossbreeds.

Crossbreeds have one large hump. They are stronger than either of their parents and can carry heavier loads. A camel uses its hump to store fat. If there is no food, its body uses the fat. The hump empties. As soon as there is food, the hump fills up again.

People say that camels store water in their humps. This is not true.

Use a word from the story to fill each space.

1 A camel with two humps is a ____________________.

2 How many humps has a crossbreed? ____________________

3 Camels store ____________________ in their humps.

4 Camels do ____________ store water in humps.

5 Which word means the same as **drains**?

____

Anagrams 1

Write the missing word in each sentence. This word is made up of all the letters in the word printed in bold type.

1 Playing tennis, Bob hit **ten** balls into the ________________.

2 I helped Mum push the ________________ up the **ramp**.

3 My **mate**, Steve, keeps a ________________ lizard.

4 A scratch from the **rose** bush made my arm ____________.

5 I had to **blow** on my ____________ of soup as it was hot.

6 The **post** is there to __________ cars parking on the lawn.

7 Mum **buys** early at the shops when they are not too

________________.

8 As the **tide** was coming in, we ________________ our

boat to a rock.

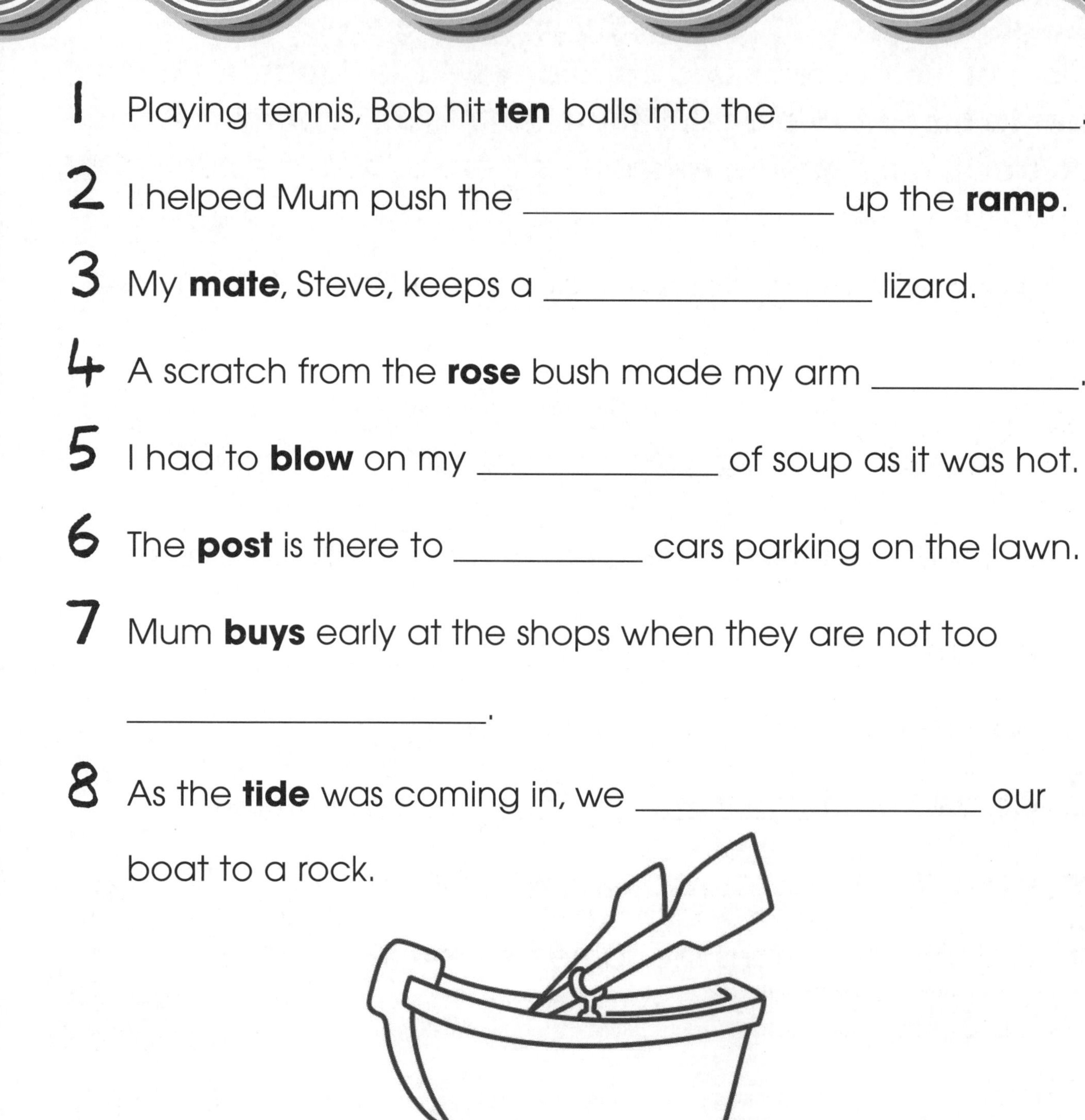

Where does tea come from?

The cup of tea we drink is made by pouring boiling water over tea leaves. They are not whole leaves, but have been dried and chopped up into small pieces. These pieces were put into packets to be sold in the shops.

Tea trees grow well in countries that are hot, but the trees need plenty of rain. The roots do not like too much water, so the trees grow well on the sides of hills where water can drain away.

Much tea is grown in India and China. There, women go picking leaves which they put into large baskets. The baskets are strapped on their backs.

Use a word from the story to fill each space.

1 We pour hot ____________________ on tea leaves.

2 Tea leaves must be chopped and ____________________.

3 Tea leaves grow on the sides of ____________________

4 In India, ________________ pick the tea leaves.

5 Which word means the same as **fastened**?

____

Which word names the group?

In each line of words one of them names the other three. Write this group word in the space.

1 shirts dresses shorts clothes ____________________

2 snacks dinners meals suppers ____________________

3 rugby cricket sport tennis ____________________

4 sweet taste sour bitter ____________________

5 wheat crop maize oats ____________________

6 rubies diamonds pearls jewels ____________________

7 ducks turkeys geese poultry ____________________

8 package parcel mail letter ____________________

9 anger feelings joy fear ____________________

10 shellfish prawns lobster oysters ____________________

What is a praying mantis?

A praying mantis is an insect. It looks as if it is praying because it holds its front legs up in front near its face.

These legs have sharp hooks for hunting. The mantis is quick to eat other insects, and will even eat any other mantis that comes along. The female mantis may turn on the male, her mate, and eat him.

Mantises are hard to see when they walk along the stem of a plant. Very often they are the same colour as the plant. No wonder an insect sometimes walks right into its jaws.

Use a word from the story to fill each space.

1 A mantis is a kind of ____________________.

2 On its legs it has sharp ____________________.

3 A female mantis might eat her ____________________.

4 A ________________ can be the same colour as a mantis.

5 Which word means the same as **difficult**?

____

Kindness should be rewarded

A wolf was eating dinner one day. He was chewing away, when suddenly he swallowed a bone. It stuck in his throat. The wolf began to howl and promised a reward to anyone who could get the bone out of his throat.

At last a stork, with its thin beak and long neck, did the job. Poking down the wolf's throat, it pulled out the bone. Then the stork asked for a reward.

'You may think yourself lucky that I did not bite your head off when it was in my mouth. Now run off, you silly stork.'

Tick the box against each sentence that is true.

1 The wolf had swallowed a bone. ☐

2 A crow tried to pull it out. ☐

3 The bone was pulled out by a stork. ☐

4 The wolf tried to eat the stork. ☐

5 The stork went off without being thanked. ☐

Missing words 2

One word is missing in each line where there are four dots. Write the word that you think should be there.

The koala is an Australian a.... . We 1 ______________

call it a bear, b.... it is really a marsupial. 2 ______________

Marsupial mothers have a p.... . This is 3 ______________

where a b.... koala lives after it is born. 4 ______________

Other m.... are kangaroos, possums and 5 ______________

wombats.

Koalas eat g.... leaves. The juice from 6 ______________

these l.... gives the animal water. It does 7 ______________

not need to d.... . 8 ______________

Koalas in the wild are k.... by pythons 9 ______________

and dingoes. Those that l.... near towns 10 ______________

may get run over by c.... or killed by pet 11 ______________

dogs. We must do our b.... to help keep 12 ______________

these harmless animals alive.

Which tree is the largest?

Although not the tallest, the banyan tree is the largest.

This tree is found in India. The trunk grows branches. As they grow, they put out hanging roots which reach the ground and grow into new stems. These stems grow thicker and thicker until the banyan tree looks like a little forest.

A banyan tree may have as many as 350 stems as thick as a normal tree. It grows little figs, which are red and are about the size of a cherry. Hundreds of bats, birds and monkeys will make a banyan tree their home. Because it is hot in India, men and women often shelter from the heat under the branches.

Use a word from the story to fill each space.

1 The banyan tree grows in ____________________.

2 Red ________________ can be gathered and eaten.

3 What four legged animals live in a banyan tree?

____

4 What keeps on growing thicker? ________________

5 Which word means the same as **ordinary**?

____

How big is the sun?

The sun is a star and the Earth is one of its planets. To get an idea of the size of the sun, we can imagine cutting it into a million pieces. One piece out of the million would still be bigger than the Earth.

If a car could be driven on a flat road right round the Earth at 80 kilometres an hour without stopping, it would take about 17 days to complete the trip. If it were possible to do the same on the sun, it would take about 5 years.

Not only is the sun very large, but it is a ball of fire and is very hot. We are not sure how hot it is, but it would be at least 100 times hotter than the Earth.

Use a word from the story to fill each space.

1 The Earth is one of the sun's __________________.

2 The sun is more than a __________________ times bigger than the Earth.

3 To travel around the __________________ at 80 kilometres an hour would take 5 years.

4 The sun is hotter than the __________________.

5 Which word means the same as **finish**?

Crossword puzzle 2

Write the answers in the puzzle using the clues below. Each word has the 'e' sound like in 'hen'. Write the answers again next to the clues.

Across

3 I can wear a ________________ round my waist.

5 A bird's home is a ________________.

7 One ________________ of a hammer is the head.

8 A wild animal may live in a ________________.

9 The crashed car was full of ________________.

Down

1 I must ________________ a letter to you soon.

2 My fishing rod broke so Dad will ________________ it.

4 I have ________________ toes.

6 When we camp I sleep in a ________________.

Why does the moon shine?

The moon shines in the sky at night. It only looks bright because the sun is shining on it. The moon travels right round our Earth once every twenty-nine and a half days.

At times we can see the whole moon. That is when the moon and the sun are on opposite sides of the Earth. At other times when the moon is between us and the sun, we can only see part of it.

The moon broke off from our world millions of years ago. Now nothing is alive on it. No wonder! At times it can be too hot or too cold. There is no oxygen to breathe.

Use a word from the story to fill each space.

1 The sun shines on the ______________.

2 Sometimes we see only ____________________ of the moon.

3 The moon was once part of our ________________________.

4 There is no _________________________ on the moon.

5 Which word means the same as **living**?

____

Change the first letter 2

The first letter of a word in each sentence is wrong. Write the word correctly in the space.

1 Try to gloat if you fall in the water. ________________

2 Mum will darn the mole in my jumper. ________________

3 He was killed by a stray pullet. ________________

4 We use fools to make things with wood. ________________

5 Dad asked me to take the leaves. ________________

6 I like to eat horn on the cob. ________________

7 The teacher told Nelly to use her drains. ________________

8 Hens sit on eggs so chicks can watch. ________________

9 We had bears and cream for dessert. ________________

10 Wendy likes to spread money on her toast. ________________

which is the largest shell?

The largest shell in the world is the giant clam. Clams live in water around coral reefs. The coast of Australia is home to this large shell.

A clam is as heavy as two large men. Its mouth may be as big as one metre wide. Divers who walk on the sea bed are always careful of these clams. There is always a chance of treading on the mouth and having a foot caught.

There are lots of smaller clams. They are dug up on beaches. In Australia one small clam that makes good bait for fishing is the pipi.

Use a word from the story to fill each space.

1 The giant clam is the largest ________________.

2 A clam has a wide ________________.

3 ________________ are afraid of clams.

4 A small Australian clam is the ______________.

5 Which word means the same as **little**?

____

Which animal is almost blind?

A mole can hardly see. It really does not need eyes, because it lives under the ground. Its small eyes are shaded by fur. It keeps them shut most of the time.

To dig long tunnels and make larger rooms for the family, a mole needs strong back legs. These have long sharp nails. The front legs, used to pull loose soil away, are more like paws. Moles eat worms and insects they find when digging.

Moles live in many countries. There are none in Australia. It is common in England to find piles of loose soil on top of a lawn. They have been pushed up by moles that have been digging below.

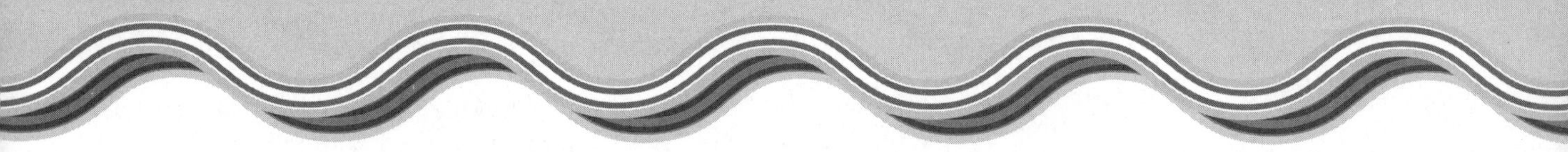

Use a word from the story to fill each space.

1 A mole keeps its eyes ____________________.

2 Its back legs are ____________________.

3 A meal for a mole is an insect or a ____________________.

4 Moles leave loose ________________ on top of lawns.

5 Which word means the same as **heaps**?

____

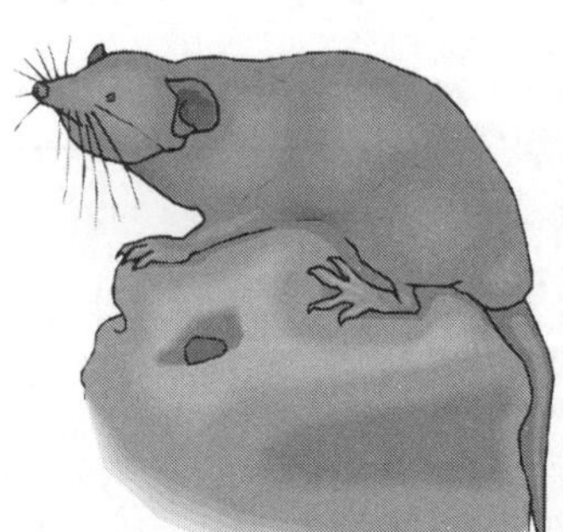

Who is speaking? 2

Read each sentence. Write who is speaking in the space. Choose answers from the box.

thief gardener jockey father

baker firefighter postal worker waiter

1 I hope my horse runs well today. ____________________

2 Keep the hose on that flame. ____________________

3 That house is easy to rob. ____________________

4 You have three letters today. ____________________

5 I shall trim that tree now. ____________________

6 Would you like to order a drink? ____________________

7 Your Mum and I have been married for ten years.

____

8 Our meat pies are fresh this morning.

____

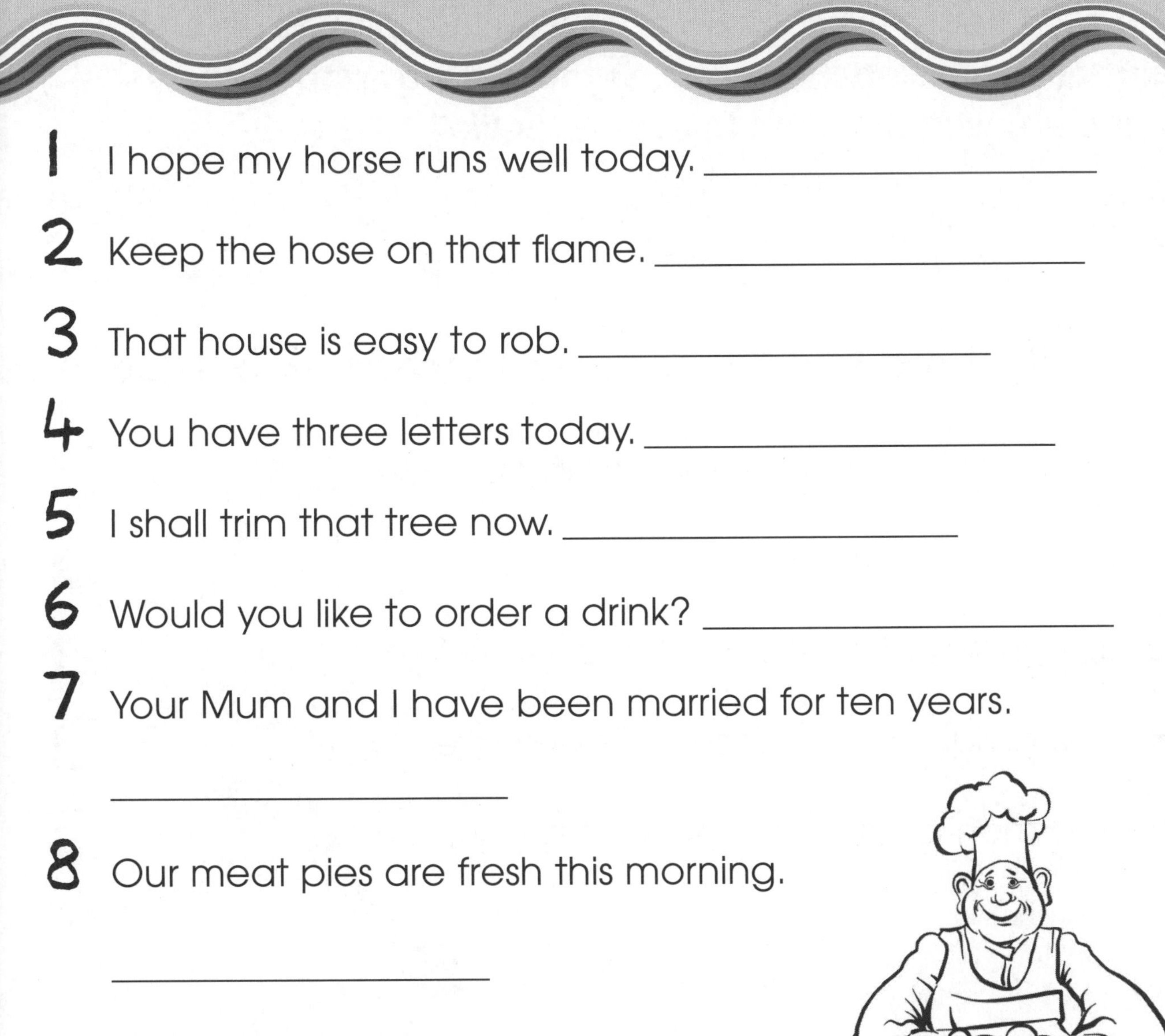

Kind people deserve thanks

One frosty day in winter, a man found a snake in his garden. The snake was almost dead from the cold.

The man took pity on the snake and carried it into the house. He put it on a rug in front of the fire. The snake soon began to wriggle. Then it started to hiss at the man's baby boy and little girl. It even wanted to bite them.

The man heard his children crying out. He picked up a stick and quickly killed the snake. 'Is this the way you treat someone who has tried to save your life?'

Tick the box against each sentence that is true.

1 It was cold when the man found a snake. ☐

2 The snake tried to bite him. ☐

3 The snake was placed on the stone floor. ☐

4 The children were afraid of the snake. ☐

5 The man killed the snake with a gun. ☐

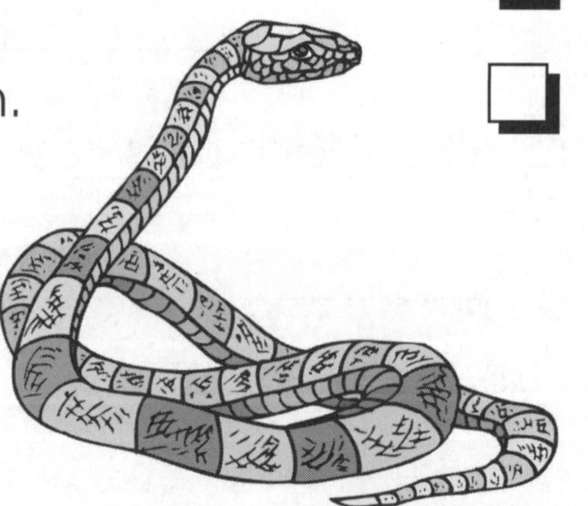

Where do shells come from?

The shells in the sea are little houses that living creatures make for themselves. They make shells to protect themselves from fishes who want to eat them.

They also have a shell to stop the water washing them around.

We call these creatures shell-fish, but a fish has bones with no shell. Shell-fish have no bones – only a soft body inside the shell.

When the shell-fish die, the empty shell is washed up on the beaches. The waves smash the shells, so if you look at a handful of beach sand you will see tiny bits of shells.

Use a word from the story to fill each space.

1 Shells are ____________________ for creatures.

2 Fish do not have a ____________________.

3 Instead, a fish has ____________________.

4 Empty shells are washed up on _______________.

5 Which word means the same as **break**?

____

Anagrams 2

Write the missing word in each sentence. This word is made up of all the letters in the word printed in bold type.

1 With one **arm** the shearer held the ________________.

2 The rat in the **trap** had eaten ______________ of the bait.

3 Uncle Bill **lost** ________________ of money at the races.

4 She sits on this **seat** as she ______________ her lunch.

5 The **foal** ate a whole ________________ of stale bread.

6 There are far too **many** Indian _____________ birds here.

7 Both cats tried to kill the **wasp** with their ______________.

8 My aunt won a **free** trip to the Barrier ________________.

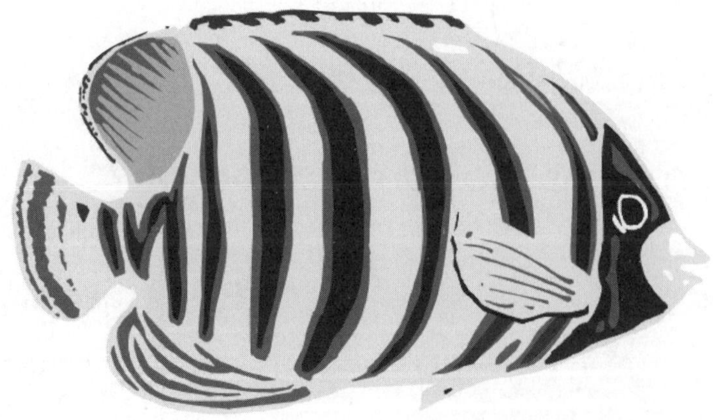

Answers

Page 1 **1** short **2** rumpy **3** round **4** rabbit **5** kind

Page 2 **1** slowest **2** down **3** leaves **4** jungle **5** rests

Page 3 **1** full **2** live **3** less **4** made **5** Towns **6** cut **7** make **8** us **9** not **10** and **11** to **12** men

Page 4 **1** lenses **2** see **3** Maggots **4** doors **5** tiny

Page 5 **1** monkeys **2** talking **3** hive **4** ant

Page 6 **1** beggar **2** driver **3** mother **4** chef **5** clown **6** farmer **7** teacher **8** nurse

Page 7 **1** horse **2** whale **3** red **4** green **5** shuts

Page 8 Tick **3** and **5**

Page 9 **Across: 2** hand **4** black **6** man **7** flap **8** gap; **Down: 1** hat **3** damp **4** bang **5** cat

Page 10 **1** tunnel **2** mixture **3** harm **4** insect **5** snatches

Page 11 **1** fish **2** pram **3** crown **4** tricks **5** butter **6** carrots **7** nasty **8** pork **9** goose **10** belly

Page 12 **1** dinosaur **2** million **3** swamps **4** tail **5** house

Page 13 Bactrian **2** one **3** fat **4** not **5** empties

Page 14 **1** net **2** pram **3** tame **4** sore **5** bowl **6** stop **7** busy **8** tied

Page 15 **1** water **2** dried **3** hills **4** women **5** strapped

Page 16 **1** clothes **2** meals **3** sport **4** taste **5** crop **6** jewels **7** poultry **8** mail **9** feelings
10 shellfish

Page 17 **1** insect **2** hooks **3** mate **4** plant **5** hard

Page 18 Tick **1**, **3** and **5**

Page 19 **1** animal **2** but **3** pouch **4** baby **5** marsupials **6** gum **7** leaves **8** drink **9** killed **10** live **11** cars **12** best

Page 20 **1** India **2** figs **3** monkeys **4** stems **5** normal

Page 21 **1** planets **2** million **3** Sun **4** Earth **5** complete

Page 22 **Across:** **3** belt **5** nest **7** end **8** den **9** dents **Down:** **1** send **2** mend **4** ten **6** tent

Page 23 **1** moon **2** part **3** world **4** oxygen **5** alive

Page 24 **1** float **2** hole **3** bullet **4** tools **5** rake **6** corn **7** brains **8** hatch **9** pears **10** honey

Page 25 **1** shell **2** mouth **3** divers **4** pipi **5** small

Page 26 **1** shut **2** strong **3** worm **4** soil **5** piles

Page 27 **1** jockey **2** firefighter **3** thief **4** postal worker **5** gardener **6** waiter **7** father **8** baker

Page 28 Tick **1** and **4**

Page 29 **1** houses **2** shell **3** bones **4** beaches **5** smash

Page 30 **1** ram **2** part **3** lots **4** eats **5** loaf **6** myna **7** paws **8** Reef

Page 31 **1** fly **2** America **3** fish **4** eagle **5** largest

Page 32 **1** heard **2** up **3** came **4** went, walked **5** had **6** car **7** speed **8** town **9** was **10** keep **11** course **12** for **13** giving

Page 33 **1** Egypt **2** stone **3** bandages **4** ropes **5** built

Page 34 **1** muscle **2** arteries **3** veins **4** blood **5** quickly

Page 35 **1** butcher **2** vet **3** pilot **4** sailor **5** cook **6** dentist **7** doctor **8** plumber

Page 36 **1** dogs **2** webs **3** instincts **4** chemicals **5** tummy

Page 37 Tick **1**, **4** and **5**

Page 38 **Across: 2** kitten **5** tick **6** little **7** ring **Down: 1** sister **3** thin **5** bit

Page 39 **1** sun **2** clouds **3** rains **4** drought **5** above

Page 40 **1** ride **2** wickets **3** mice **4** mate **5** Bitter **6** porch **7** roses **8** dingo **9** flood **10** cough

Page 41 **1** solid **2** Dunlop **3** air **4** pump **5** softer

Page 42 **1** fangs **2** glands **3** tree **4** crush **5** stored

Page 43 **1** eat **2** able **3** snow **4** aunt **5** palm **6** rare **7** meals **8** lemon

Page 44 **1** leaves **2** longer **3** spots **4** kick **5** baby

Page 45 **1** road **2** car **3** centre **4** lamps **5** break

Page 46 **1** watch **2** dead **3** sour **4** lord **5** gone **6** near **7** done **8** steak **9** though **10** pear

Page 47 **1** Sydney **2** wave **3** dolphin **4** friend **5** lies

Page 48 **1** gone **2** down **3** up **4** said **5** Baba **6** gold **7** and **8** saw **9** take **10** bags **11** them **12** home

Page 49 **1** watches **2** Africa **3** black **4** ostrich **5** fastest

Page 50 **1** tail **2** air **3** cells **4** lungs **5** drop

Page 51 **1** convict **2** pianist **3** priest **4** actor **5** mechanic **6** poet **7** tailor **8** shearer

Page 52 **1** France **2** God **3** English **4** killed **5** battle

Page 53 **1** brain **2** up **3** remember **4** current **5** under

Page 54 **Across: 1** cot **2** spots **5** dog **6** docks **Down: 1** clock **3** pond **4** trod

Page 55 **1** grass **2** lions **3** horses **4** gallop **5** close

Page 56 Tick **1**, **3**, **4** and **5**

Page 57 **1** heard **2** said **3** really **4** window **5** bed **6** Brer **7** dead **8** lift **9** come **10** leg **11** loud **12** ran

Page 58 **1** beak **2** America **3** fruit or fruits **4** hollow **5** remain

Page 59 **1** teeth **2** tongue **3** claws **4** knuckles **5** strange

Page 60 **1** years **2** man **3** made **4** not **5** Tell **6** set **7** hit **8** was **9** hundred **10** cut **11** two **12** killed

Page 61 **1** under **2** periscope **3** tanks **4** water **5** sea

Page 62 **1** first **2** health **3** wheat **4** America **5** guests

Page 63 **Across: 1** gum **4** jump **6** nuts **7** uncle **Down: 2** money **3** sun **5** pup **7** tug

Page 64 **1** eggs **2** snake or cobra **3** India **4** hood **5** bushy

Which is the largest bird?

The largest bird is the ostrich. It has a big body and long bony legs. This makes it so heavy that it cannot fly. It can only run fast along the ground.

The largest bird that can fly is the condor from South America. Its wings spread out to three metres. This bird is a kind of vulture. It feeds on dead animals. Sometimes it catches fish from rivers or lakes with its feet.

Another very large bird, nearly as large as the condor, is the eagle. The wedge-tailed eagle from Tasmania is the largest of all the eagles.

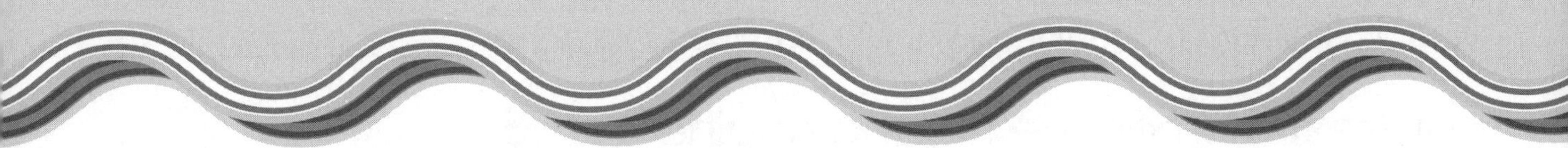

Use a word from the story to fill each space.

1 The ostrich is too heavy to ____________________.

2 The largest flying bird lives in South ____________________.

3 A condor can catch ____________________.

4 A wedge-tail is an ______________.

5 Which word means the same as **biggest**?

____

Missing words 3

One word is missing in each line where there are four dots. Write the word that you think should be there. This page is adapted from the book *Wind in the Willows* by Kenneth Grahame.

Half way through his meal Toad h.... 1 ____________

the sound of a car pulling u.... at the 2 ____________

hotel. Some people c.... inside. 3 ____________

Toad slipped out and w.... up to the 4 ____________

car. Next moment he h.... the engine 5 ____________

going. He swung the c.... around and 6 ____________

drove off. He increased s.... and raced 7 ____________

out of the t.... and onto the highway. 8 ____________

He w.... the mighty Toad once more. 9 ____________

Everyone must k.... out of his way. 10 ____________

Of c.... Toad was caught. He was given 11 ____________

one year for stealing, three f.... speeding 12 ____________

and fifteen for g.... cheek to the police. 13 ____________

What are the pyramids?

Three large pyramids still stand in Egypt. They were built a few thousand years ago. Each pyramid was made of many huge blocks of stone. The largest pyramid was about 150 metres tall.

All this stone was used to hide the bodies of dead kings or queens. Each body was wrapped in bandages and put in a hollow part of the pyramid. We call these bodies mummies. They were left with food, drink and other things he or she might need to get to the next life.

Many workers were used to build these three large pyramids. They used ropes to push and pull the very large stone blocks into place.

Use a word from the story to fill each space.

1 The pyramids are in ____________________.

2 A pyramid was made of ____________________ blocks.

3 A king's body was wrapped in ____________________.

4 The stones were pulled with ________________.

5 Which word means the same as **made**?

____

What is your pump?

Your heart is your pump. Its walls are made of muscle. Day and night it pumps blood. Some goes up to your brain. Some goes all the way down to your toes.

The important part about pumping is that blood must come in and then out of your lungs. There it picks up oxygen to feed cells in the body, and the waste matter from cells is taken out of the blood.

The fresh bright red blood that leaves your heart flows along arteries. The dirty darker blood comes back to your lungs in veins. If you cut an artery or a vein you must quickly stop the bleeding. It is dangerous to lose too much blood.

Use a word from the story to fill each space.

1 Your heart is made of ______________________________.

2 Clean red blood travels along ________________________.

3 Dirty dark blood travels along ________________________.

4 We must not lose too much __________________________.

5 Which word means the same as **hurriedly**?

____

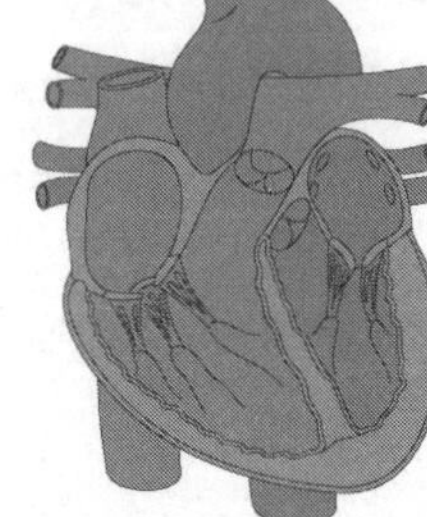

Who is speaking? 3

Read each sentence. Write who is speaking in the space. Choose answers from the box.

cook	**vet**	**doctor**	**plumber**
sailor	**pilot**	**butcher**	**dentist**

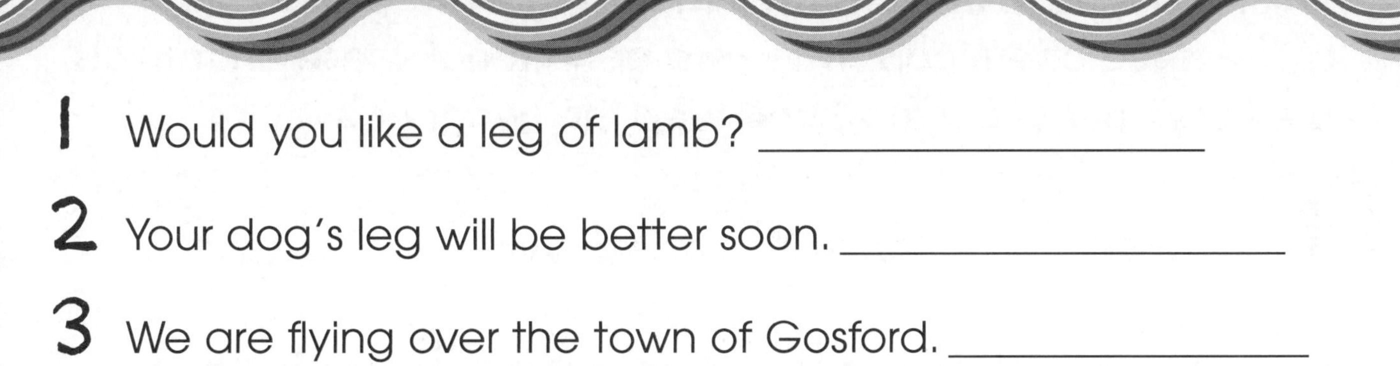

1 Would you like a leg of lamb? ____________________

2 Your dog's leg will be better soon. ____________________

3 We are flying over the town of Gosford. ____________________

4 I don't like being at sea in a storm. ____________________

5 The cake is ready to put in the oven. ____________________

6 Open wide and let me see your teeth. ____________________

7 You feel better after taking some pills. ____________________

8 I have come to fix your taps. ____________________

What makes us hungry?

Animals do things without being taught. Dogs dig holes to bury bones. Cats wash by licking their fur. Birds make nests. Spiders spin webs. They all do this by what we call instinct.

Humans have few instincts. They have to be taught. One instinct that we are not taught is to feel hungry.

As soon as there is too little food in our body, we have a sinking feeling in the tummy. It means that the cells in our blood need chemicals. When we eat a meal, these chemicals are taken out of our food and feed the hungry cells.

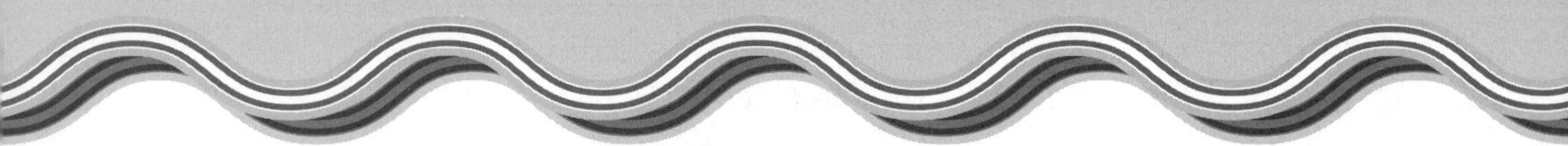

Use a word from the story to fill each space.

1 Bones are buried by ______________________.

2 Spiders are able to spin ______________.

3 Humans do not have many ________________.

4 Cells use the __________________ found in food.

5 Which word means the same as **stomach**?

____

Be happy with who you are

A crow was not at all happy with his plain black feathers. He felt that the parrots with their blue, red, pink or green feathers were lucky.

The crow went looking for parrots' feathers that had fallen out. He soon found a few red and blue feathers. He managed to fasten them on his back.

The next day the crow saw parrots in some trees. They were pink and white galahs. He flew to them. The parrots soon saw the visitor was a crow. They chased him away. He flew back to his friends, but they would not speak to him again.

Tick the box against each sentence that is true.

1 The crow did not like black feathers. ☐

2 The crow wanted white feathers. ☐

3 The crow found green and blue feathers. ☐

4 The galahs chased the crow away. ☐

5 The crow upset his other crow friends. ☐

Crossword puzzle 3

Write the answers in the puzzle using the clues below. Each word has the 'i' sound like in 'ink'. Write the answers again next to the clues.

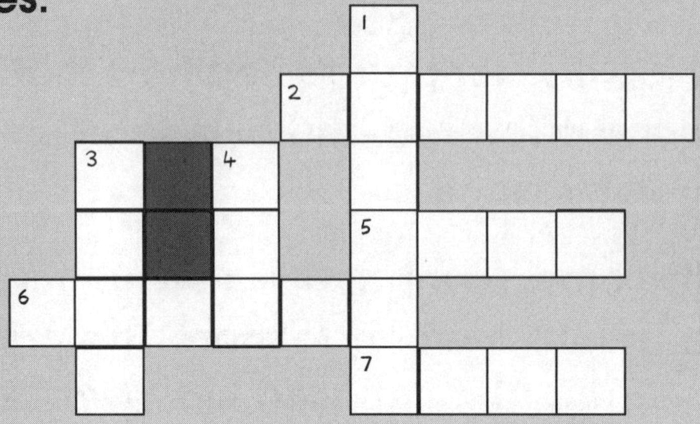

Across

2 A baby cat is a ____________________.

5 You can hear some clocks ____________________.

6 A fish that is not big is ____________________.

7 Mum has a gold ____________________ on her finger.

Down

1 My brother is Mick and my ____________________ is Jane.

3 A lamb that is fat is not ____________________.

4 The bird ____________________ my finger and made it bleed.

Where does rain come from?

When the sun shines, water is sucked up into the air.

The water comes mainly from the seas. It can also come from rivers. Water even goes into the air from the clothes when washing on the clothesline dries.

When there is a lot of water in the air it forms into dark clouds. Clouds can become full of heavy drops of water. When it rains, the clouds above are dropping water.

Pools, ponds and lakes lose water whenever the sun shines. They can be filled again with rain water. If there is no rain for a long time we call it a drought.

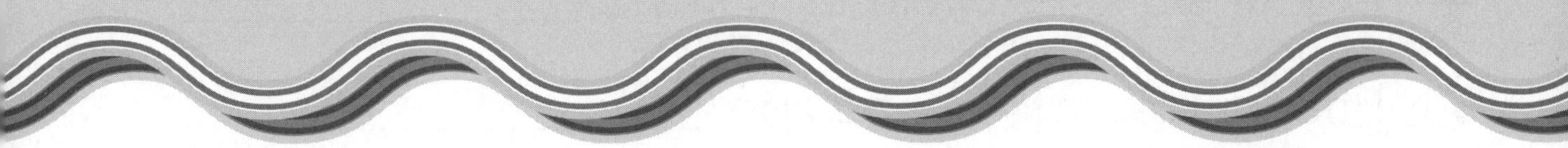

Use a word from the story to fill each space.

1 Water is sucked into the air by the hot ________________.

2 Water in the air turns into dark ________________.

3 When clouds drop water it ________________.

4 A long time with no rain is a ______________.

5 Which word means the same as **overhead**?

____

Change the first letter 3

The first letter of a word in each sentence is wrong. Write the word correctly in the space.

1 My sister can hide her bike without falling. ________________

2 The bowler took six tickets in the game. ________________

3 Cats chase after rice and may eat them. ________________

4 A gate is another word for a friend. ________________

5 Litter apples may not be ripe. ________________

6 The two girls sat on the torch and talked. ________________

7 She grows pink noses in her garden. ________________

8 A bingo is a wild dog that kills sheep. ________________

9 Very heavy rain caused the blood. ________________

10 The chemist sold us some rough mixture. ________________

Who first made pump-up tyres?

The first bicycles had tyres made of solid rubber. If you rode a bicycle for a long time your body was shaken. No wonder you felt sore. The solid tyres bumped and jolted along the roads.

Luckily, over a hundred years ago, John Dunlop changed all this. He had an idea that tyres could be filled with air. This would make a softer ride.

John made two tubes. The tube for the inside of the tyre was filled with air. The other outer tube was the tyre itself that ran along roads. Since then, cars, trucks, planes and other things with wheels have pump-up tyres.

Use a word from the story to fill each space.

1 The first bicycles had ________________ rubber tyres.

2 It was John ________________ who changed this.

3 His inner tube was filled with ________________.

4 Planes have ______________-up tyres.

5 Which word means the same as **gentler**?

____

How do poisonous snakes bite?

A snake has two pointed front teeth called fangs. We also have two pointed teeth, but they are different.

The snake's fangs have a little channel running down one side. This allows poison to run into anything the snake bites. The poison is made and stored in two glands in the snake's mouth. The glands squirt the poison along the teeth.

Not all snakes carry poison. Many tree snakes are harmless. Large and small pythons do not need poison. They can coil round and crush an animal before swallowing it.

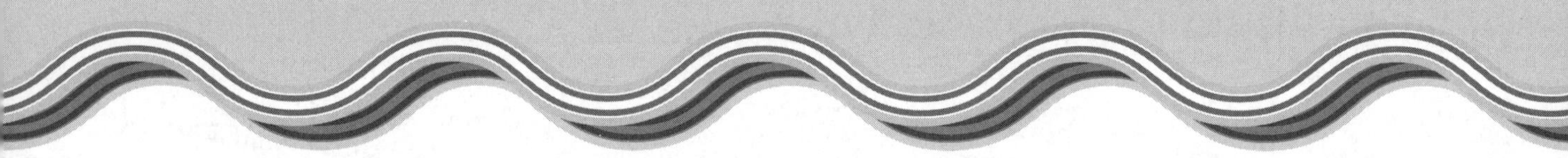

Use a word from the story to fill each space.

1 The pointed teeth of snakes are called ________________.

2 The poison is kept in ________________.

3 ________________ snakes do no harm.

4 Pythons ______________ and eat animals.

5 Which word means the same as **kept**?

____

Anagrams 3

Write the missing word in each sentence. This word is made up of all the letters in the word printed in bold type.

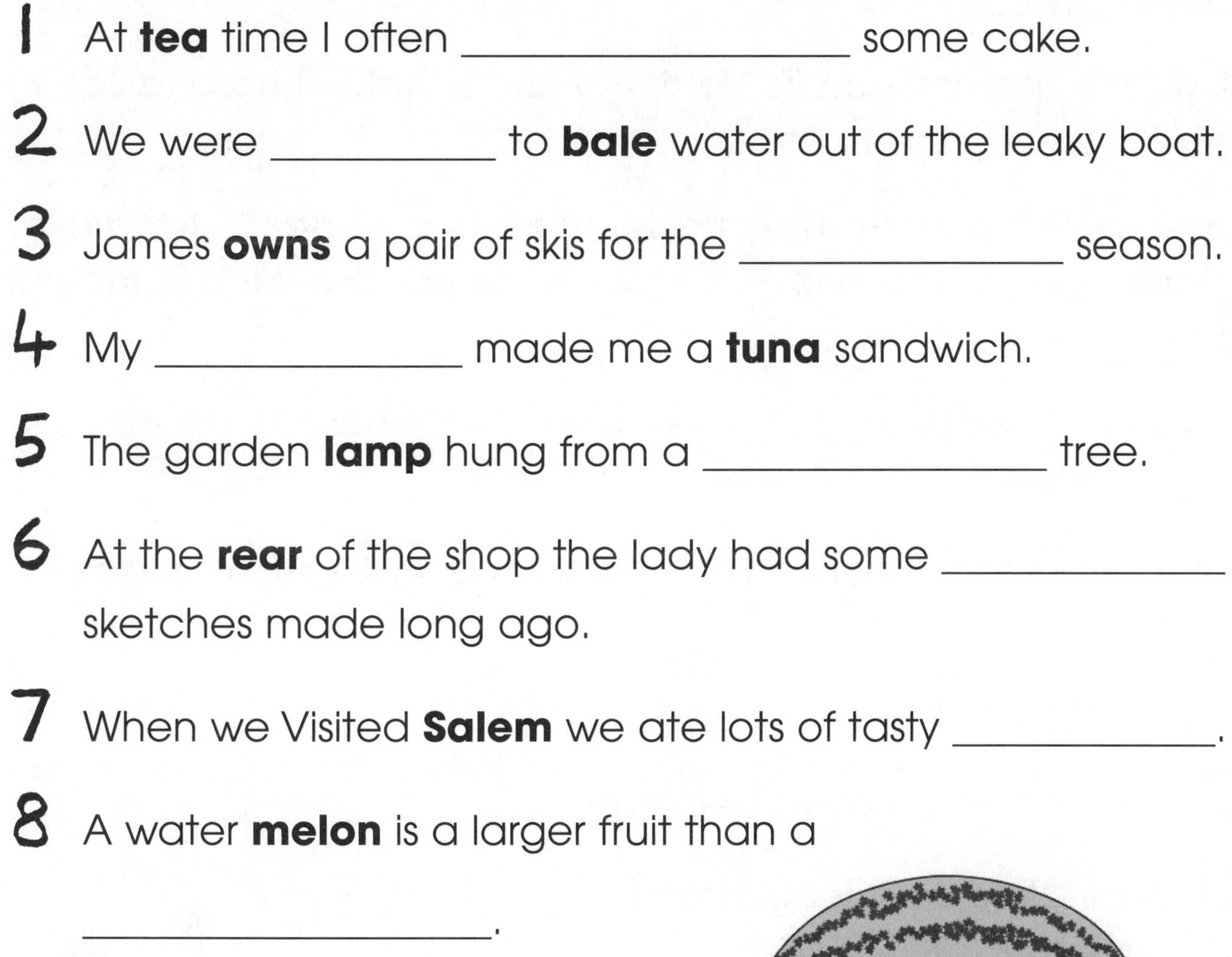

1 At **tea** time I often ____________________ some cake.

2 We were ___________ to **bale** water out of the leaky boat.

3 James **owns** a pair of skis for the ________________ season.

4 My ________________ made me a **tuna** sandwich.

5 The garden **lamp** hung from a ________________ tree.

6 At the **rear** of the shop the lady had some _______________ sketches made long ago.

7 When we Visited **Salem** we ate lots of tasty ______________.

8 A water **melon** is a larger fruit than a

_____________________.

Which is the tallest animal?

The tallest animal is the giraffe. Many other animals in Africa eat grass, but the giraffe eats leaves. It has to stretch up to find the best leaves.

Very slowly, over thousands of years, giraffes' necks have become longer and longer. They have had to reach higher and higher.

A giraffe has spots on its coat. The spots make it hard to see the giraffe among the trees.

Lions attack giraffes. They prefer to kill baby ones. A full grown giraffe has very long legs. It can kick hard. One kick in the right place could kill a lion.

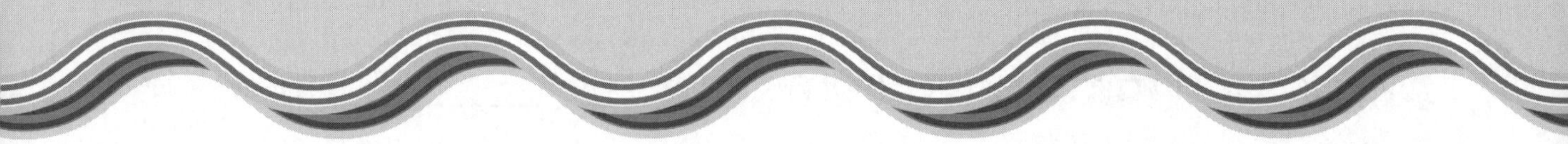

Use a word from the story to fill each space.

1 Giraffes mainly eat ______________________.

2 Giraffes' necks have become ______________.

3 A giraffe's coat is covered in __________

4 A __________________ from a giraffe could kill a lion.

5 Which word means the same as **young**?

____

What are cat's eyes?

Yes, we know that a cat sees with its eyes but there are other kinds of cat's eyes. These cat's eyes are made of glass and a tiny mirror fitted into an iron frame. The frame, in a rubber cushion, is sunk into the road.

Car tyres can run over them. They do not break. They just squash down a little and pop up again.

Usually the cat's eyes are placed three or four metres apart. They may mark the centre or edge of a road. Drivers switch on the headlights at night. The cat's eyes shine brightly in the beams. There is no need for street lamps. The drivers know just where they are going.

Use a word from the story to fill each space.

1 Cat's eyes are placed side by side on a ________________.

2 Tyres from a ________________ can pass over the eyes.

3 Eyes can be on the edge or in the ________________.

4 Street ______________ are not needed.

5 Which word means the same as **shatter**?

____

Which words do not rhyme?

Read each group of five words. Write the one word that does not rhyme with the other four.

1 catch latch match watch hatch ____________________

2 feed bead dead seed read ____________________

3 four soar war sour door ____________________

4 lord word bird third herd ____________________

5 bone moan gone shown blown ____________________

6 pear swear chair near dare ____________________

7 flown lone shown loan done ____________________

8 cheek beak speak steak peek ____________________

9 though bough cow meow now ____________________

10 deer weir near steer pear ____________________

It does not pay to tell lies

In 1888, a sailing ship was caught in a storm near Sydney. A huge wave crashed over the ship. The sailors only had time to jump into the sea before the ship sank. The crew's pet monkey also ended up in the water.

A dolphin swimming by offered to take the monkey to dry land on its back. On the way, the dolphin asked the monkey, as a joke, if he knew Governor Phillip. 'Oh, yes! I know him well. He is a friend of mine,' replied the monkey.

The dolphin knew then that the monkey was a liar. It was a hundred years since Governor Phillip came to Sydney with the First Fleet. The dolphin then dived below the ways and left the monkey in the sea.

To tell lies is one way of ending up in deep water.

Use a word from the story to fill each space.

1 The ship was sailing near ____________________.

2 What made the ship sink? A ____________________.

3 What creature offered to save the monkey? ______________

4 The monkey said Governor Phillip was his ________________.

5 The dolphin did not like anyone who told

____________________.

Missing words 4

One word is missing in each line where there are four dots. Write the word that you think should be there. This page is adapted from 'Ali Baba and the Forty Thieves'.

As soon as the thieves were g...., Ali Baba 1 ____________

climbed d.... from the tree. He walked 2 ____________

u.... to the small door in the rock. 'Open, 3 ____________

Sesame!' s.... Ali Baba. 4 ____________

At once the door opened wide. Ali B.... 5 ____________

stepped into a cave. There he saw g...., 6 ____________

silver, jewels a.... rich cloth. He was 7 ____________

amazed at what he s.... . 8 ____________

Ali Baba decided to t.... some bags of 9 ____________

gold for himself. He put these b.... on 10 ____________

his donkeys, covered t.... with sticks and 11 ____________

went h.... to his wife. 12 ____________

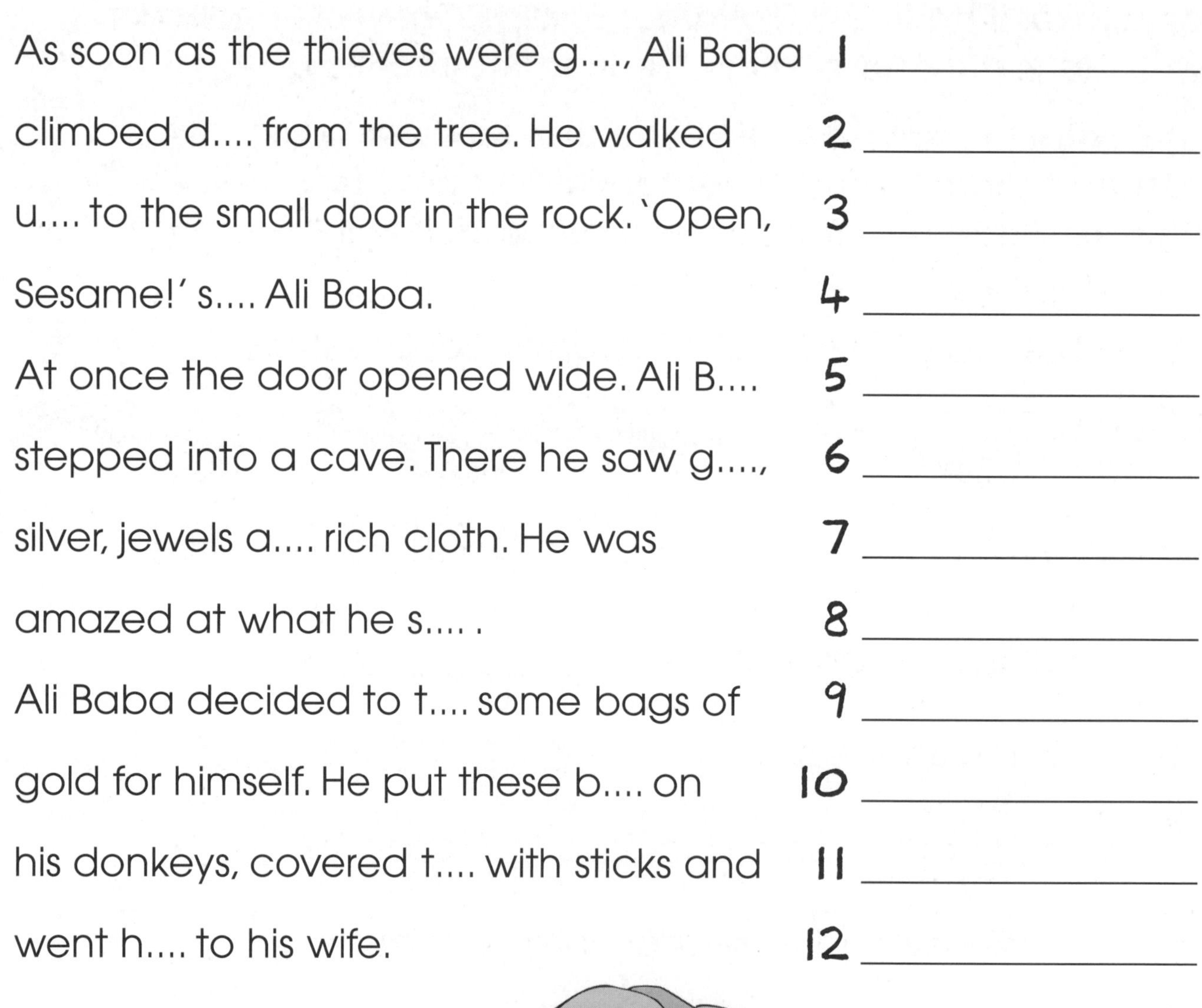

Which animals run the fastest?

The speed of animals has been timed with stop watches. The fastest animal was the cheetah. This spotted African cat can run at about 100 kilometres an hour. It cannot keep up this great speed for long. It may be able to run as fast as this for a minute or so.

A cheetah crawls slowly towards its prey. Its tummy and head scrape along the ground. The black spots on its sandy coat help it to blend in with rocks and bushes. It then springs and runs at full speed to bring down animals for a meal. It chases and kills rabbits, wild pigs, all kinds of deer and even baby ostriches.

Use a word from the story to fill each space.

1 Stop ______________ timed the speed of animals.

2 Cheetahs live in ______________.

3 A cheetah's coat is sandy with ______________ spots.

4 One young bird cheetahs like is the ______________.

5 Which word means the same as **quickest**?

____

What happens to tadpoles' tails?

A tadpole swims in water but does not breathe air. Later it turns into a frog. We all know that a frog has no tail. So a tadpole must lose its tail to become a frog. Does it just drop off? Is it bitten off by frogs?

No! The tadpole has cells in its body that slowly eat up its own tail. It might take a little while, but the tail gets smaller and smaller until there is none.

Other changes take place. The tadpole grows legs, and lungs replace gills. Now it can breathe air and be a frog that swims in water and hops on land.

Use a word from the story to fill each space.

1 A frog has a head but no ________________.

2 At first a tadpole does not breathe ________________.

3 A tadpole's tail is eaten by tiny ________________.

4 A tadpole has gills and grows ______________ to breathe.

5 Which word means the same as **fall**?

____

Who is speaking? 4

Read each sentence. Write who is speaking in the space. Choose answers from the box.

priest	**convict**	**actor**	**poet**
shearer	**mechanic**	**pianist**	**tailor**

1 I want to be set free from this prison. ____________________

2 I played for an hour at the concert. ____________________

3 Welcome to my church! ____________________

4 In the play I am a princess. ____________________

5 Your car needs a new fan belt. ____________________

6 I am trying to find a word that rhymes. ____________________

7 I have finished the suit you ordered. ____________________

8 There is a lot of wool on these sheep. ____________________

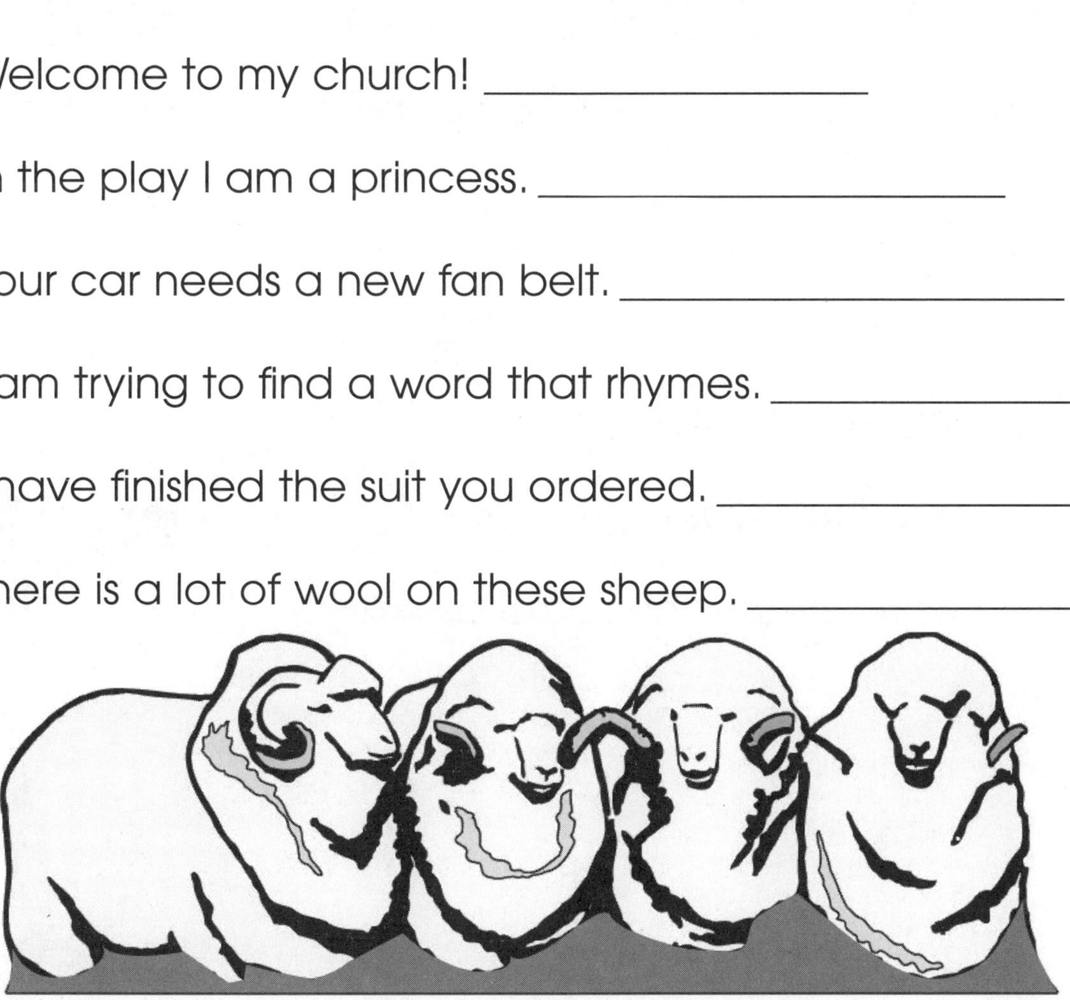

Who was Joan of Arc?

Joan of Arc was a young French girl. She lived in France. Much of France was ruled by an English king. The French wanted their own king to rule over France.

Joan heard a voice from God telling her to lead a French army. She rode a horse and led the army into battle. At first the French beat the English, but in the end she was captured. People were very cruel in those days. The English wanted Joan to say that she did not hear from God. They said that only witches heard voices. Joan would not obey. So they tied her to a post and killed her by burning. Joan later became a saint.

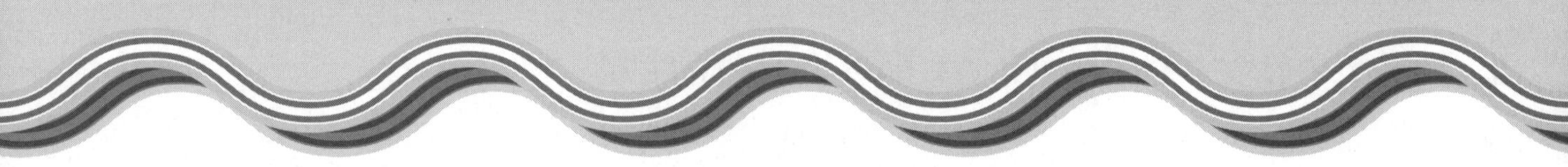

Use a word from the story to fill each space.

1 Joan of Arc lived in ________________.

2 She heard a voice from ________________.

3 Joan went to fight the ________________

4 In the end Joan was ______________.

5 Which word means the same as **war**?

____

What does a worm know?

Worms live under the ground. There are more worms than people in the world.

A worm has no brain but it seems to be able to think. It knows to come up when the ground is very wet.

It has even been proven that worms can remember. In a test, a tunnel was made with a T junction at the end. The worms could turn either left or right to find food but a small electric current was put in the left-hand passage. The worms were taken out but they would never turn left for their food again, even when there was no current.

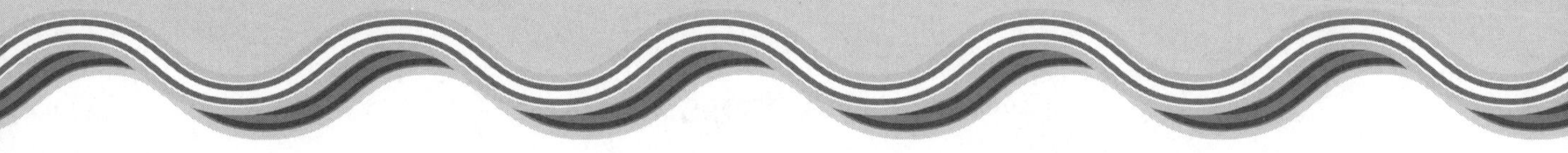

Use a word from the story to fill each space.

1 A worm can move but has no ________________.

2 In wet weather worms come ________________.

3 A test proved that a worm can ________________.

4 An electric ______________ was used.

5 Which word means the same as **below**?

____

Crossword puzzle 4

Write the answers in the puzzle using the clues below. Each word has the 'o' sound like in 'dog'. Write the answers again next to the clues.

Across

1 Baby sleeps in a ____________________.

2 Sally was ill with red ____________________ on her face.

5 Bob has a ____________________ that barks at cats.

6 Ships are tied up at the ____________________.

Down

1 We can tell the time from a ____________________.

3 Ducks like to swim on a ____________________.

4 Jane ____________________ on some glass and cut her foot.

Why has a zebra stripes?

Zebras live in Africa. They feed on grass which often grows tall. If they were all white, or all black, there would be few zebras left. Nearly all of them would be killed by lions. It would be too easy for these big cats to see them in the long grass.

Instead, the zebra has, over thousands of years, grown a special coat. It has black and white stripes that blend with tall grass. A lion has to come close before it sees zebras. These animals, like horses, hear and smell well. They can sense that a lion is nearby. Often the zebras are able to run away as they can gallop very fast.

Use a word from the story to fill each space.

1 Zebras eat ____________________.

2 In Africa, zebras are eaten by ____________________.

3 What other animals are like zebras? ____________________

4 Which word tells how a zebra runs? ________________

5 Which word means the same as **near**?

____

Nobody likes a traitor

In Australia there is a wild dog – the dingo. Farmers set traps for the dog because it kills sheep.

One day a farmer came to a trap and found a live dingo caught by its foot. It had only been in the trap a few hours.

'Let me go, and I will lead my friends, one by one, into your trap,' said the dingo. 'That is all the more reason why I should shoot you,' replied the farmer. 'You are not a loyal dog. You should be ashamed if you are willing to betray your friends just to save your life.'

Tick the box against each sentence that is true.

1 A dingo lives in the wild. ☐

2 One dingo was caught by its neck in a trap. ☐

3 The dingo offered to help the farmer. ☐

4 The dingo made matters worse for itself. ☐

5 The farmer probably shot the dingo. ☐

Missing words 5

One word is missing in each line where there are four dots. Write the word that you think should be there. This page is adapted from *Tales of Uncle Remus* by Joel Chandler Harris.

Brer Rabbit h.... that Brer Fox was dead. 1 ________________

So Brer Rabbit s.... he had better go and 2 ________________

see if Brer Fox was r.... dead. 3 ________________

Looking through the w...., Brer Rabbit 4 ________________

saw Brer Fox lying stiff in b.... . He went 5 ________________

up close to Brer Fox. 'That's funny. B.... 6 ________________

Fox is d.... , but doesn't act dead. 7 ________________

Dead people l.... their hind legs and shout 8 ________________

'Wahoo!' when visitors c.... ,' said Brer 9 ________________

Rabbit. Just then Brer Fox lifted his l.... 10 ________________

and said 'Wahoo!' in a l.... voice. 11 ________________

Brer Rabbit r.... for his life. 12 ________________

Why has the toucan a huge beak?

The toucan is a brightly coloured jungle bird. The strange thing about this bird from South America is its beak. It seems too long and fat for its body.

But there is a reason. The toucan lives on fruits that grow at the tips of very thin twigs. The heavy bird cannot sit on the twigs as they would snap off. It is too heavy to flap its wings and remain near the fruit like a humming bird.

Instead, the toucan can sit on a thicker twig and stretch its long bill and pick fruit. No, the bird does not topple over from the weight of its beak. The beak is made up of hollow tubes inside a light outer covering.

Use a word from the story to fill each space.

1 The toucan has a strange ____________________.

2 This bird lives in South ____________________.

3 It likes to eat ____________________.

4 The ______________ tubes make the beak light.

5 Which word means the same as **stay**?

____

Which animal has no teeth?

The ant-eater's mouth is like a long tube. There are no teeth inside. In its mouth is a long tongue that looks like a worm. This tongue, coated with sticky spit, can slide in and out. The ant-eater pokes its tongue into ants' nests. The unlucky ants sticks to the outside of the tongue and are gobbled up by the ant-eater.

This strange animal has huge claws on its front feet. They are used for digging at a fast pace into ants' nests. When the ant-eater walks, it tucks the front claws under its foot and walks on its knuckles.

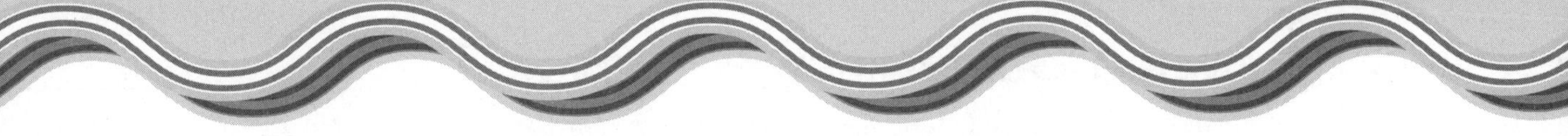

Use a word from the story to fill each space.

1 An ant-eater has no ________________.

2 In its mouth is a very long ________________.

3 Ant-eaters have very large ________________.

4 Ant-eaters walk on their front ____________.

5 Which word means the same as **odd**? ________________

Missing words 6

One word is missing in each line where there are four dots. Write the word that you think should be there.

Many y.... ago Swiss people were ruled 1 ______

by a wicked m.... named Gessler. He put 2 ______

his hat on a pole and m.... people bow 3 ______

to it. William Tell would n.... bow. 4 ______

Tell was arrested. Gessler knew T.... was a 5 ______

hunter. He promised to s.... Tell free if he 6 ______

shot and h.... an apple placed on the 7 ______

head of Tell's son. The boy w.... to stand 8 ______

a h.... yards away. Tell took two arrows. 9 ______

One c.... the apple in half. Gessler asked 10 ______

Tell why he had t.... arrows. 'The other 11 ______

one was for you if I k.... my son,' said Tell. 12 ______

How does a submarine work?

A submarine is made of iron. It floats like a ship. It also has one or more propellers. A submarine can dive down and move under water. If it is not down deep, the captain can use the periscope to see above the water. Submarines are used to attack other ships.

To sink down, water is sucked into special tanks. This makes the submarine heavier until it is under the waves. Once it is under, it is quite like a fish and can move forward. To come up again, a button is pressed and the water is pumped out of the special tanks. The submarine becomes lighter and comes up out of the sea.

Use a word from the story to fill each space.

1 A submarine moves on and ____________________ water.

2 Sailors look out through a ____________________.

3 To go down ____________________ fill with water.

4 To come up the ______________ is pumped out.

5 Which word means the same as **ocean**?

____

When did we first eat cereals?

Breakfast is the first meal of the day. For many years the rich ate bacon and eggs with toast. The poor may have had bread and cheese.

In America, just over 100 years ago, Doctor John Kellogg and his brother William ran a health farm.

One day for breakfast, the guests were given a cereal made from wheat flakes. When it was mixed with milk, everybody liked this new breakfast dish.

Before long, the brothers made corn flakes which also tasted good. Kelloggs corn flakes were put in packets and sold all over America. They still sell well all over the world today.

Use a word from the story to fill each space.

1 Breakfast is the ____________________ meal of the day.

2 The Kellogg brothers ran a ____________________ farm.

3 The Kelloggs first made ____________________ flakes.

4 Shops sold Kelloggs flakes in ______________.

5 Which word means the same as **visitors**?

____

Crossword puzzle 5

Write the answers in the puzzle using the clues below. Each word has the 'u' sound like in 'bug'. Write the answers again next to the clues.

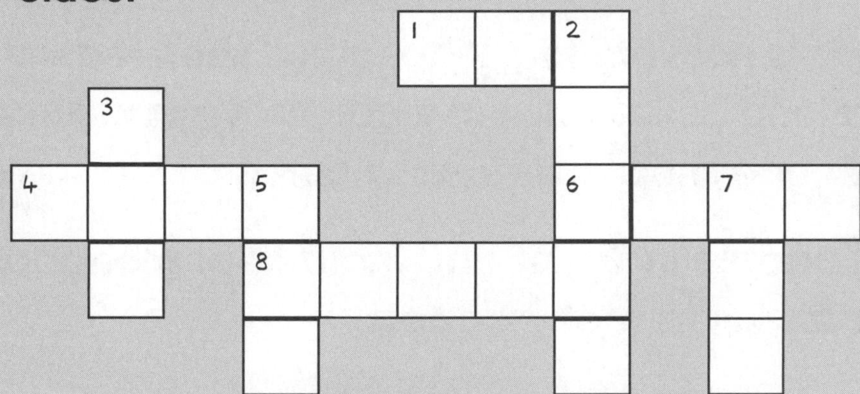

Across

1 There are many ________________ trees in Australia.

4 A frog will ________________ as it moves along.

6 Monkeys like to eat ________________.

8 My Mum's brother is my ________________.

Down

2 We need ________________ to buy things.

3 The ________________ shines in the sky.

5 A baby dog is a ________________.

7 A ________________ pulls or pushes ships.

What animal kills snakes?

Snakes keep away from a mongoose. This small animal likes nothing better than a snake for dinner. In the wild, it also feeds on birds, birds' eggs and lizards.

A mongoose is not very big. It has small short legs, a pointed nose and a long bushy tail. But it can move and jump sideways quickly. With one snap of its jaws, it can crack a snake's skull.

Years ago, people in Egypt and India kept mongooses as pets. These animals killed many cobras.

The cobra is a very dangerous snake. It has a large hood around its head.

Use a word from the story to fill each space.

1 A wild mongoose eats bird's ____________________.

2 A mongoose will kill a poisonous ____________________.

3 People in Egypt and ________________ often kept a mongoose.

4 The cobra's head has a ________________.

5 Which word means the same as **furry**?

____